J
793.8
FUL

Fullman, Joe.
    Mind tricks.

Magic
HANDBOOK

MIND TRICKS

Joe Fullman

QEB Publishing

Published in the United States by
QEB Publishing, Inc.
23062 La Cadena Drive
Laguna Hills, CA 92653

www.qeb-publishing.com

Library of Congress Control Number: 2008010191

ISBN 978 1 59566 607 9

Printed and bound in United States

Author Joe Fullman
Editor Amanda Askew
Designer Jackie Palmer
Illustrator Mark Turner for Beehive Illustrations

Publisher Steve Evans
Creative Director Zeta Davies

Picture credits
Alamy Mary Evans Picture Library 11 and 15
Corbis Christopher Farina 22
Getty Images Ethan Miller 18 and 31
Rex Features 9, 17, Charles Sykes 29
Shutterstock Donald R Swartz 7

Contents

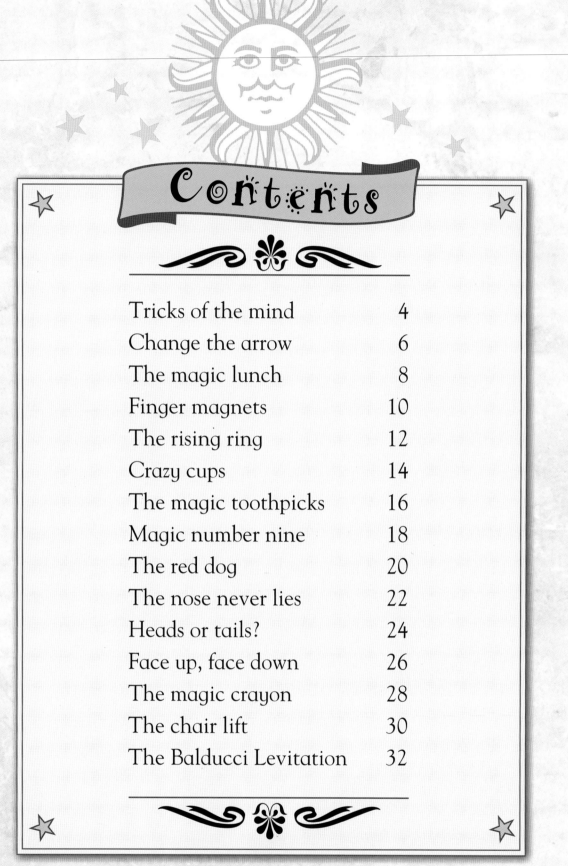

Tricks of the mind	4
Change the arrow	6
The magic lunch	8
Finger magnets	10
The rising ring	12
Crazy cups	14
The magic toothpicks	16
Magic number nine	18
The red dog	20
The nose never lies	22
Heads or tails?	24
Face up, face down	26
The magic crayon	28
The chair lift	30
The Balducci Levitation	32

Tricks of the mind

Mind tricks are different to other kinds of trick. With most magic tricks, it is obvious that the magician is using their skills to fool the audience. Part of the fun is that the magician often tries to convince the audience that there is no trickery involved. Instead they make it look like they are using strange powers to read the volunteer's mind.

① Preparation

Sometimes you may need to prepare part of the trick before you start your performance.

Putting on a show

Mind tricks are all about the performance. The better you perform your tricks, the more your audience will believe that you have special powers. Mind tricks often work best in ordinary locations, such as a living room or on a street corner, where your audience is less likely to be suspicious about being tricked.

② Difficulty rating

The tricks get harder throughout the book, so each trick has been given a rating. One is the easiest and seven is the hardest. The most difficult tricks will take a bit of practise to get right, but the results will be worth it!

Change the arro

Use water to magically change the direction of the arrow. This trick is simple, but very impressive.

①

Preparation

• Before facing your audience, place your card and glass on the table.

• Fold the card in half. On one side of the card, draw an arrow. It should be just shorter than the width of your glass.

1

③ Props needed...

The props you will need throughout the book.

- A pack of playing cards, known as the deck. Each pack should contain 54 cards—two Jokers plus four suits of 13 cards. The suits are Spades, Clubs, Diamonds, and Hearts.
- Banana
- Book or magazine
- Bowl
- Calculator
- Card

- Coins
- Deck of playing cards
- Elastic band
- Soda in a glass bottle
- Glasses/cups
- Jug of water
- Lunchbox
- Metal ring
- Needle and thread

- Packet of wax crayons
- Paper
- Pencils
- Pin
- Stool
- Table
- Toothpicks or cocktail sticks
- Dishwashing liquid
- Watch

② Place a glass in front of the arrow, so the arrow can be clearly seen through the glass.

③ Now challenge your audience to make the arrow change direction without touching the paper or glass.

④ **Stages and illustrations**

Step-by-step instructions, as well as illustrations, will guide you through each trick.

④ When they give up, produce your hidden jug of water and pour it into the glass. The arrow will appear to change direction. Pouring the water will turn the glass into a lens and, from the audience's viewpoint, change the direction of the arrow.

⑤ **Top Tip!**

Hints and tips help you to perform the tricks better!

Making the Statue of Liberty disappear

⑥ In 1983, the magician David Copperfield performed one of the most amazing illusions of all time when he made the 305-foot Statue of Liberty disappear in front of a New York audience. No one knows for sure how the did it, but some people believe the audience were sat on a revolving turntable. When the statue was briefly hidden behind drapes, the turntable turned away from the statue. The curtain was then dropped, revealing empty space.

▶ The "reappeared" Statue of Liberty— David Copperfield has never told anyone how he made it "vanish."

⑥ **Famous magicians and illusions**

Find out who are the most exciting and skillful magicians, and what amazing feats they have performed.

Change the arrow

Use water to magically change the direction of the arrow. This trick is simple, but very impressive.

Props needed...
* Glass
* Jug of water
* Pencil
* Table
* Thin piece of card

Preparation

• Before facing your audience, place your card and glass on the table.

• Fold the card in half. On one side of the card, draw an arrow. It should be just shorter than the width of your glass.

1 Stand your folded piece of card on the table with the arrow facing the audience.

Top Tip!

Always speak clearly when talking to your audience, so they can understand what you are saying and what is happening.

2 Place a glass in front of the arrow, so the arrow can be clearly seen through the glass.

Now challenge your audience to make the arrow change direction without touching the paper or glass.

Making the Statue of Liberty disappear

In 1983, the magician David Copperfield performed one of the most amazing illusions of all time when he made the 305-foot (93-meter) Statue of Liberty disappear in front of a New York audience. No one knows for sure how the did it, but some people believe the audience were sat on a revolving turntable. When the statue was briefly hidden behind drapes, the turntable turned away from the statue. The curtain was then dropped, revealing empty space.

▶ The "reappeared" Statue of Liberty— David Copperfield has never told anyone how he made it "vanish."

4 When they give up, produce your hidden jug of water and pour it into the glass. The arrow will appear to change direction. Pouring the water will turn the glass into a lens and, from the audience's viewpoint, change the direction of the arrow.

The magic lunch

Performed well, these two tricks will make your friends think that you have a magic genie in your lunchbox.

Preparation

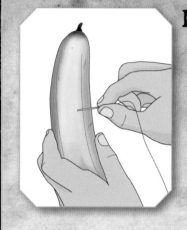

* Push the threaded needle into one of the ridges and out through the next ridge.

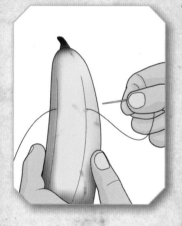

* Push the needle back into the second hole and out through the third ridge. Make sure a loop of thread hangs out of the banana.

* Repeat until you've been all the way round. Then pull both ends of thread out through the first hole and this will slice the banana. Repeat as many times as you like.

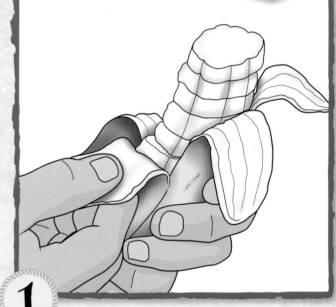

1 Tell your friend that you think you have a "genie" in your lunchbox. To prove it, open your lunchbox and hand your friend the banana. Ask them to peel it. The banana will come apart in slices in their hands. The genie did it!

Top Tip!
The more you act as if what you are doing is "magic" and not part of a trick, the more your audience will believe you.

Preparation

Place your glass bottle of soda in the refrigerator for several hours so that it is very cold.

1 Take the bottle of soda out of your lunchbox. Open it and hand it to your friend and tell them that the genie is trying to get out. Put the coin on top of the bottle to keep the genie in.

2 Tell your friend to hold onto the bottle with both hands. After a while, the coin will pop up slightly, "letting the genie out." As long as the bottle is cold enough, the warmth of your friend's hands will cause the gas inside the bottle to expand, pushing the coin up.

Crazy stunts

Criss Angel often performs amazing stunts to a shocked audience! He has been run over by a steamroller while laying on a bed of glass, and even escaped being hit by a speeding car—while chained to a parked car full of explosives. Criss sometimes reveals to his fans how his illusions are done.

▶ In 2002, Criss Angel hung from eight fish-hooks for nearly six hours!

Finger magnets

★ ★

Props needed...
* Watch

This fascinating routine uses a very important mind trick technique—the power of suggestion. You will make your volunteer believe that something natural is happening by the power of magic!

1 Ask a volunteer if you can hypnotize them. Tell them that it is safe and the effect will only last for a couple of minutes.

2 Now pretend to hypnotize them. Wave a watch in front of them and ask them to follow it with their eyes.

3 Now, ask them to clasp their hands together.

4 Keeping their other fingers together, ask them to stick up their first fingers.

Using magic to end a war

In the 19th century, France controlled the African country of Algeria. Fearing that the people there were going to start a war against them, the French government sent the magician Robert-Houdin to Algeria. He performed many amazing magic tricks, including catching a bullet between his teeth, which made the Algerian people believe that he had magic powers. This made them give up their plans for war.

▶ Feathers fly as Robert-Houdin, the "magician who stopped a war" performs one of his many amazing tricks.

5 Tell your volunteer that when you hypnotized them, you magnetized their fingers. Wave your hands over their fingers and tell them that no matter how hard they try to keep their first fingers apart, the magnetism will draw them together.

Top Tip!

Tell jokes or stories while doing your trick to misdirect, or distract, your audience from what you're actually doing. Then they won't work out how the trick is done!

6 Watch as your volunteer's fingers slowly start moving together. As you have told them that they are hypnotized, they will think that is why their fingers are touching. In fact, when held in this position, your fingers will naturally come together.

The rising ring

Watch in amazement as the ring seems to defy gravity with this simple trick.

Props needed...
* Elastic band
* Metal ring

Preparation
Cut your elastic band so that it is a single length of elastic.

Top Tip!
When performing a trick, try to appear confident. Act as if you know exactly what you are doing, even if you don't. The more nervous you seem, the more the audience will feel that you are trying to trick them.

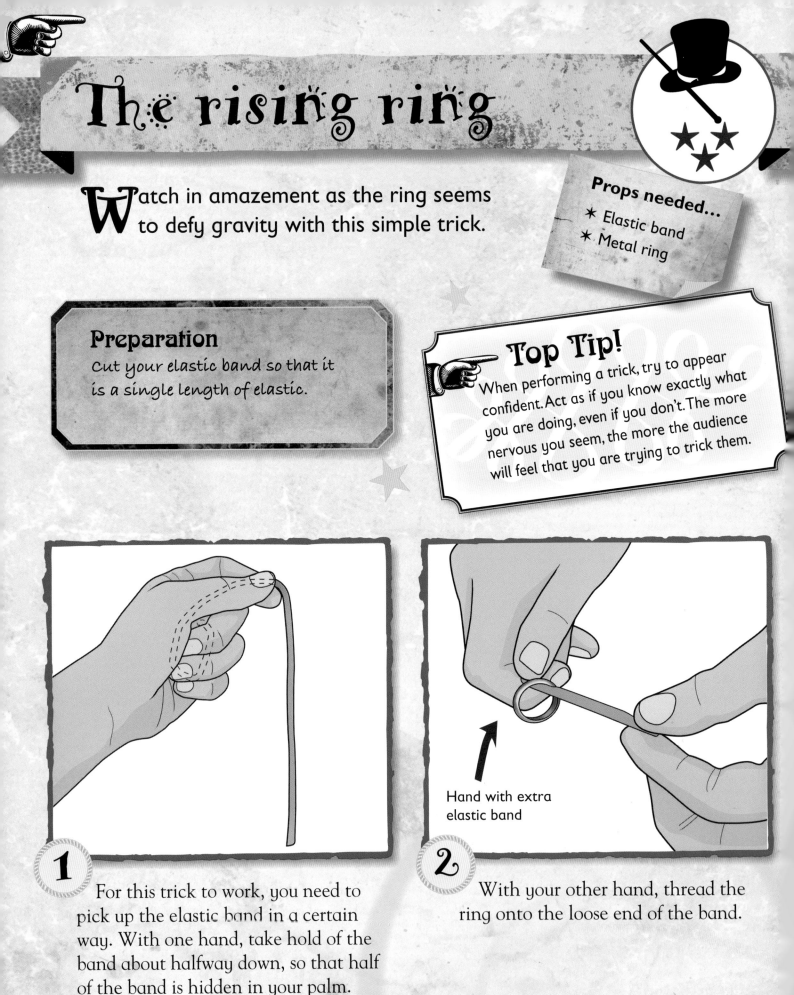

Hand with extra elastic band

1 For this trick to work, you need to pick up the elastic band in a certain way. With one hand, take hold of the band about halfway down, so that half of the band is hidden in your palm.

2 With your other hand, thread the ring onto the loose end of the band.

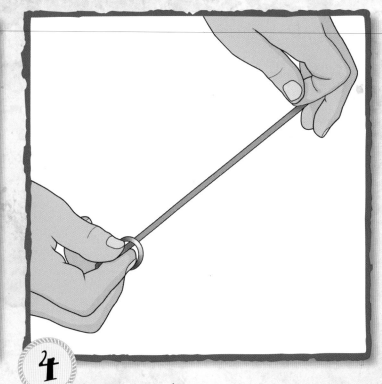

3 Grip the loose end of the band and pull it taut. Show the audience that there is nothing suspicious about the ring by raising and lowering your hands to slide the ring up and down.

4 Announce that you are going to make the ring defy gravity. The ring should rest against the hand hiding the length of elastic. Lift your other hand so that the band is now stretched into a slight slope.

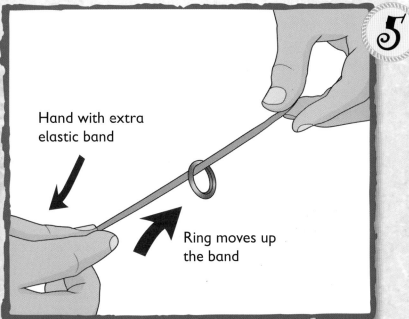

Hand with extra elastic band

Ring moves up the band

5 Now for the tricky bit. Slowly and carefully, let the length of elastic band gathered in your hand slip through your finger and thumb. This will make it look like the ring is magically sliding up the band. In fact, it is being carried upward by the elastic band, although your audience will not notice this.

Crazy cups

Props needed...
* Three cups

Here is a trick guaranteed to drive your audience crazy. As simple as it looks, no matter how hard they try, they just will not be able to get it to work.

Preparation

Set up the cups in this way.

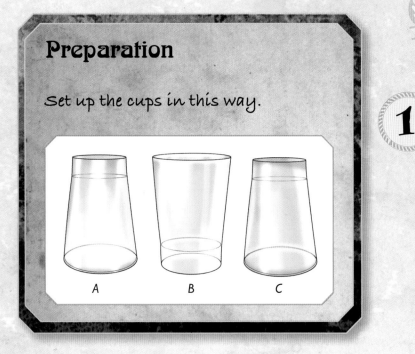

A   B   C

1 Tell a volunteer that you want them to turn the cups the right way up. Explain that they can turn them just three times, and that each time they must turn two cups at once, one with each hand. First, show your volunteer how it is done.

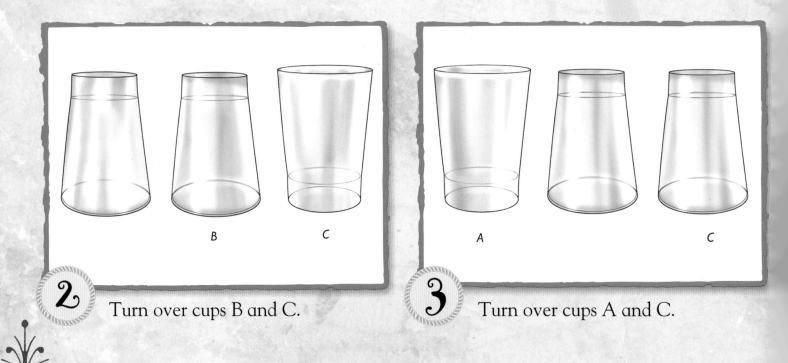

2 Turn over cups B and C.

3 Turn over cups A and C.

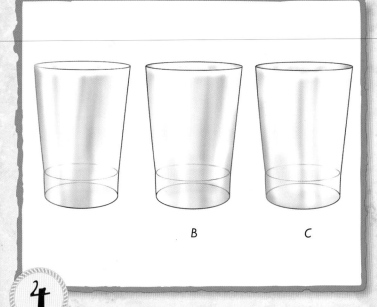

B   C

Top Tip!

Make sure you set up the cups for your friend as quickly and as casually as possible, so they cannot see that you are tricking them. Once you have completed step 4, you only need to turn over the middle cup.

4 Turn over cups B and C again.

The heaviest box

In his stage act, the 19th-century magician Robert-Houdin would get a child to pick up a lightweight metal box. He would then challenge a strong man from the audience to do the same. When the man was unable to lift it, Houdin would claim it was because he had used magic to make them lose their strength. In fact, he had secretly turned on a powerful magnet, which held the box to the floor.

A   B   C

5 Now reset the cups for your volunteer to try the trick. However, when you set up the cups for them, you are going to do it slightly differently. Although it may look similar, the way you set up the cups for your volunteer is in fact opposite to the way you do it for yourself.

▶ Robert-Houdin often used his son in his act, as in this levitation trick.

The magic toothpicks

You will need to gather your audience around you to perform this trick—you will not be able to move your props once they are set up.

Props needed...
* Small bowl
* Toothpicks or cocktail sticks
* Dishwashing liquid
* Water

Preparation

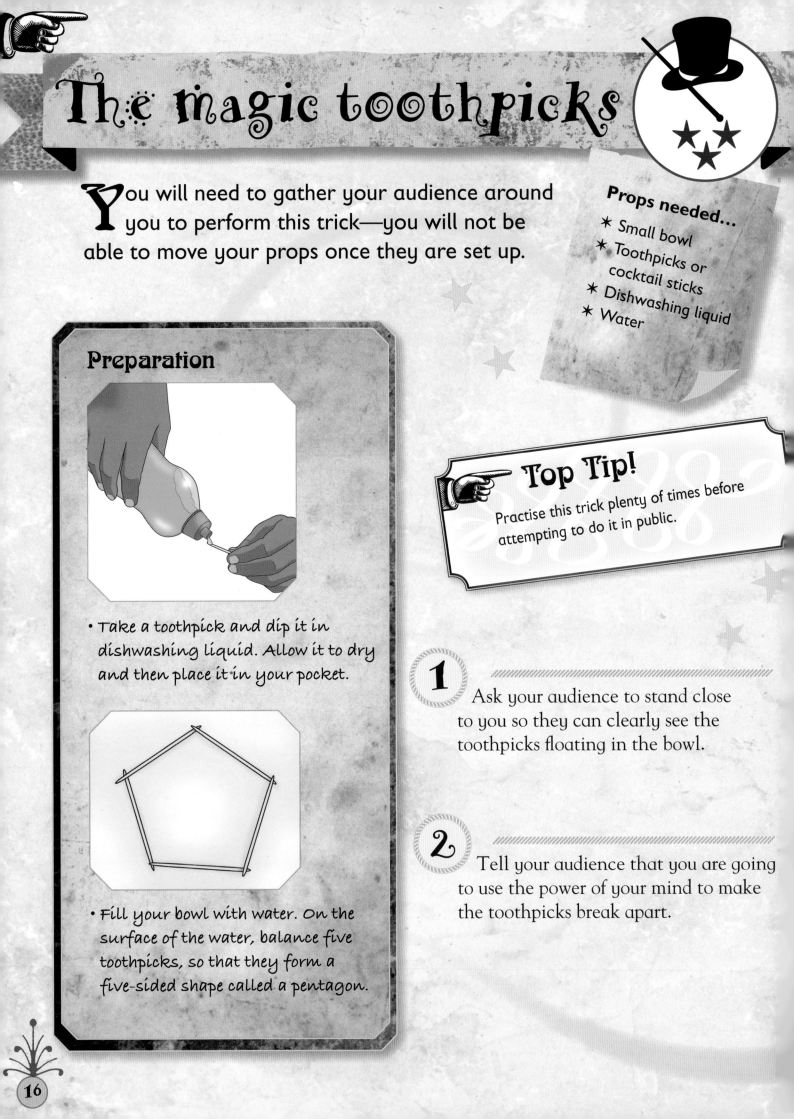

* Take a toothpick and dip it in dishwashing liquid. Allow it to dry and then place it in your pocket.

* Fill your bowl with water. On the surface of the water, balance five toothpicks, so that they form a five-sided shape called a pentagon.

Top Tip!

Practise this trick plenty of times before attempting to do it in public.

1 Ask your audience to stand close to you so they can clearly see the toothpicks floating in the bowl.

2 Tell your audience that you are going to use the power of your mind to make the toothpicks break apart.

3 Take out the prepared soapy toothpick from your pocket, and touch it on the surface of the water in the center of the toothpicks.

4 After a few seconds, the toothpicks forming the pentagon will begin to float away from each other.

5 Make the toothpick pentagon again and invite a volunteer to try to break it apart. Without the special soapy toothpick, they will not be able to. The dishwashing liquid on the toothpick causes a thin film of soap to form on the surface of the water. When it reaches the pentagon, the soap breaks apart the water molecules holding the toothpicks in position.

Mind magician

Derren Brown is a mind magician who uses mind-control skills and hypnotism to make people perform extraordinary acts. In his shows, he has convinced someone that they were living inside a video game, made a group of people rob a bank, and put a member of the public into a trance in one country, and then woken them up in another.

▶ *Look into his eyes—Derren Brown is one of the most popular mind magicians performing today.*

Magic number nine

You are going to use a clever piece of preparation to make it look as if you have read the mind of your subject. As long as your volunteer works out their sums correctly, this trick should work every time.

Preparation

For the best results, this trick should be performed in a casual setting, such as a living room, where there are books and magazines. Before you start the trick, choose a book or magazine, turn to page nine, and memorize the first word.

Speed magic

Hans Klok is a Dutch magician who regularly performs in Las Vegas, the "world capital of magic." He claims to be the fastest magician in the world, and packs dozens of tricks into his act, including levitation, sawing a woman in half, and making a light bulb magically float over an audience.

▶ In his act, Hans Klok performs an illusion in which he appears to separate someone's head from their body.

1 Tell your friend that you are going to read their mind. Give them a pencil, a piece of paper, and a calculator to work out any sums.

a) 4217

b) 1472

c) 4217 – 1472 = 2745

d) $2 + 7 + 4 + 5 = 18$

$$1 + 8 = 9$$

2 a) Ask your volunteer to think of a four-digit number and write it down.
b) Rearrange those four digits to make another four-digit number. Write that down as well.
c) Using the calculator, subtract the smaller number from the larger number. Write the new number down.
d) Add the four separate digits of the new number together.

3 Ask your volunteer if they have a one-digit or two-digit number. If they have a two-digit number, they need to add the digits together so they end up with a one-digit number.

4 Now ask your friend to pick up your prepared book. Ask them to turn to the page matching their final number and to memorize the first word on that page.

5 Pretend to concentrate deeply for a few moments, and then write down the word on a piece of paper and hand it to the volunteer. The secret is the number will always be nine, so you will never be wrong!

The red dog

Props needed...
* Calculator
* Two pencils
* Two pieces of paper

This trick can go wrong because it relies on your volunteer giving the most common answers. Of course, they may give other answers. However, this trick really can make you look like a mind reader.

1

Give your friend or volunteer a piece of paper and a pencil. Tell them that you are going to get them to write down a series of words. You are then going to use your mind-reading ability to work out what the words are.

a) 3

b) 3 × 9 = 27

c) 2 + 7 = 9

d) 9 − 5 = 4

Top Tip!

Rather than writing down your answers straightaway, try writing something else first, and then crossing it out, as if you are having a problem reading your volunteer's mind.

2

a) Ask them to pick a number between two and nine.
b) Multiply that number by nine—they can use a calculator if they need to.
c) Add the two digits together to make a one-digit number.
d) Subtract five from that number.

Once they have their final number, tell them that you are going to ask them some more questions, and that you want them to write their answers on a piece of paper. After each answer, concentrate on the face of your volunteer, as if you are reading their mind. Then write your own answers on a piece of paper.

4 = D

4

Whatever number they have, ask your volunteer to go to that letter of the alphabet. So, if they have 1, they would go to A, if the number is 2 they would go to B, and so on.

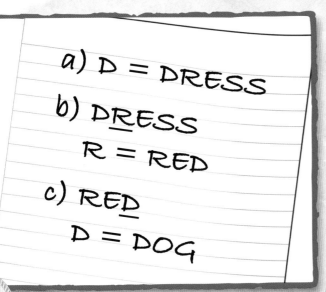

a) D = DRESS

b) D<u>R</u>ESS
   R = RED

c) RE<u>D</u>
   D = DOG

5

a) Ask them to write down an item of clothing beginning with the first letter.
b) With the second letter of that word, they should write down a color.
c) With the last letter of that word, they should write down the name of a pet.

6

Once they have finished, you can reveal your answers, which should match theirs—dress, red, dog. Certain sums always result in the number nine. By then taking away five, your volunteer should end up with the number four, and the letter "D."

The nose never lies

This trick may not work every single time, but it should work often enough to convince people of your magical powers.

Props needed...
 * Coin

Roller coaster ride

In 1999, U.S. magician Lance Burton performed a death-defying trick when he had himself handcuffed to the tracks of a roller coaster. Traveling up to 80 miles (130 kilometers) an hour, a roller coaster was set in motion on the track, giving Burton one minute to set himself free. He escaped with just a tenth of a second to spare.

▼ *Lance Burton performs another daring feat of escapology—breaking free from a straitjacket during one of his shows.*

1 Ask your friend or volunteer to put a coin in one of their hands.

2 Now ask them to put their hands behind their back, place the coin into whichever hand they want, and close their fist over it.

3

Ask them to put their closed hands in front of them. Look closely for a visual clue, which magicians call a "tell"— a movement made by your volunteer, which lets you know where something is. Most people point their nose slightly toward whichever hand the coin is in.

4

Pretend to read their mind, then tell them which hand the coin is hidden in.

5

If you have got it right, your volunteer will be impressed, but of course, it could just be luck. So you need to do the trick a few times. As long as your volunteer is doing what you want them to do, this trick should keep working.

Top Tip!

Make sure you do not let your volunteer see you staring too closely at their nose. This may make them suspicious, causing them to change their behavior.

Heads or tails?

Props needed...

* Six coins

Tell your friend, or better a group of friends, that you can predict if a coin is showing heads or tails when it is hidden beneath one of their hands.

1
Give your friends six coins, or even better, get them to provide their own six coins. If they use their own coins, they cannot think that you are using "magic coins."

2
Ask one of your friends to throw the coins onto a table so they land with some of the coins showing heads and some showing tails. If they all show heads or tails, ask them to do it again.

3
Silently count how many coins are showing heads, and note whether it is an odd number or an even number.

4
Turn your back and ask your friend to pick one coin with their left hand and one with their right hand and to turn over the coins. Tell them that they can do this with as many pairs of coins as they like, as many times as they like.

5 When they have finished turning over the coins, ask them to cover up one coin with their hand.

6 Turn back, and again make a mental note of how many of the coins are showing heads, and whether it is an odd number or an even number.

7 a) Now for the tricky bit. If you saw an odd number of heads at the beginning and it is still an odd number, or if you saw an even number and it is still an even number, the coin under the hand will be tails.

b) If the number of heads has changed, from odd to even, or from even to odd, the coin under the hand will be heads.

Face up, face down

Props needed...
* Deck of playing cards
* Table

This mind-reading trick takes quite a bit of concentration from both you and your volunteer, but it will have a big impact.

1 Ask your volunteer to hold the deck of cards face down.

2 Turn your back and ask your volunteer to count out between ten and 30 cards face up. They should remember how many cards they have dealt.

3 Your volunteer should now have two piles of cards—one face down and one face up. With your back still turned, ask them to mix the face up cards into the face down pile. They can shuffle the cards as many times as they like.

4

Your volunteer should now be holding one pile of cards—some face up, some face down. Ask them to remember how many cards they dealt out at the start of the trick and then deal out the same number of cards again.

5

Tell them to pick up the pile they have just dealt and to turn their back. Ask them to count how many of the cards in their deck are face down, but not to tell you because you are going to read their mind to find out the number.

6

Turn back to your volunteer and pick up the other pile. Silently count how many face up cards there are. If your volunteer has followed the stages correctly, the number of face up cards in your pile will be exactly the same as the number of face down cards in their pile.

7

Put down your pile, take your time to build up the tension, and then reveal the number.

The magic crayon

Props needed...
* Packet of wax crayons

This X-ray vision trick needs your best acting skills—and will only work if you don't bite your nails!

1 Hand your volunteer the wax crayons. Tell them that you can "see" colors through your fingers and you are going to tell them which color crayon they have chosen without looking.

2 Turn away from the volunteer and put your hands behind your back.

3 Ask your volunteer to pick any color crayon they want and to place it into one of your hands.

5 Now, use one of the nails on your other hand to scrape off a tiny amount of crayon with your nail.

4 With your hands still behind your back, turn round to face your volunteer.

28

Top Tip!

Telling jokes and stories will make your performance fun and distract your audience from working out what you are doing.

6 Keep the hand holding the crayon behind your back and bring the other hand up to your forehead, as if you are trying to concentrate. Curl the fingers inward and you will be able to quickly glance at the piece of crayon beneath your nail.

7 After a short pause to build up the tension, reveal the color of the crayon.

Magic in the air

Wouter Bijendijk—who performs under the stage name "Ramana" —is a renowned magician from Holland. He is particularly well known for his feats of levitation —making objects fly through the air and even appearing to hover more than 3 feet (one meter) above the ground himself.

▶ Ramana's levitation act seems particularly impressive because he often does it out on the streets, so people can see he is not using strings or wires.

29

The chair lift

Props needed...
* Stool

Reveal your friends' hidden strength with this great hands-on trick. You will need an audience for this trick because five people will take part.

1 Ask a volunteer to sit on the stool. Arrange the other four people next to them—two on the right-hand side, and two on the left-hand side.

2 Ask the four standing people to clasp their hands together and to point their index fingers forward. Tell them that they are going to try to lift the sitter into the air just using their fingers. Make it clear that you don't think this will work.

3 Two people should put their fingers in the sitter's armpits, and the other two should put their fingers behind the sitter's knees.

4 Now ask them to try to lift the sitter. They will soon find that it is impossible.

6 Wave your hand in front of the sitter's face and tell them that you are using hypnotism to make them lighter.

7 Tell the lifters that you are going to count to three. When you get to three you want them to quickly take their hands off the sitter and to try to lift them again.

5 Now tell the sitter that you are going to use mind magic to make them lighter. Ask the four lifters to all gently place their hands on top of the sitter's head.

Here's how it's done...

Penn and Teller are a special type of double act. Not only do they perform numerous clever illusions, they also spend part of each performance showing the audience exactly how some of their tricks are done.

▼ *They may look dangerous, but Penn and Teller's tricks are carefully rehearsed so that neither of them get hurt.*

8 Count to three, they start to lift and, "hey presto," the sitter is suddenly up in the air. By telling people that they can do this trick, it makes them believe that they can, so they will try harder without realizing! Also, as they are trying the second attempt at speed, they will be using more force.

The Balducci Levitation

Ere is a quick piece of mind magic you can do, known as the Balducci Levitation. Performed well, it will look to a spectator as if you have hovered in mid air for a few seconds.

1 Get your spectator to stand behind you at around a 45-degree angle. Lift the foot closest to the spectator into the air by a couple of inches.

2 At the same time, stand on the tiptoe of the other foot and lift the heel into the air by a couple of inches. You'll now look as if you are floating!